Molahs Shalom

Until I Learn To Pray

Lillie Bailey and Marilyn Bailey

AuthorHouse™
1663 Liberty Drive
Bloomington, IN 47403
www.authorhouse.com
Phone: 1-800-839-8640

Available at local bookstores and online at www.UntilILearnToPray.com or
http://www.authorhouse.com/Bookstore/BookHome.aspx

Complimentary music CD and Book can be ordered from the website www.UntilILearnToPray.com

First published by AuthorHouse 3/17/2011

ISBN: 978-1-4520-8883-9 (sc)

Library of Congress Control Number: 2010917684

Printed in the United States of America

Certain stock imagery © Thinkstock.

This book is printed on acid-free paper.

authorHOUSE®

Acknowledgements

A call to serve prompts us to acquiesce in all matters concerning our relationship with God. When we think we need help, in a twinkling of an eye we see angels waiting on every turn prepared to assist as if they had a script that we knew not of: All we can say is "Look to God".

Perseverance and Faith are our strongholds to kindle Love among a community of believers. With a passion to reach the four corners of the earth delivering His message, we are grateful to God for the cooperation of our family, permission granters, soldiers for Christ, the Jachin and Boaz, and our band of angels that made this book complete.

Heartfelt Thank Yous to ….

RBC Ministries with Ed Rock at RBC.org - "Our Daily Bread"
"The Daily Word", Grand Rapids, Michigan
Zondervan Publishers, 5300 Patterson Avenue, Grand Rapids, Michigan
Rabbi M.Munk, Wisdom in the Hebrew Alphabet *by permission*

Mesorah Publications, New York

First Baptist Church, Members and Friends, Cullen, Louisiana

Sons and Brothers: Willie White, Otis Bailey and Reece Bailey

Southern California Golden Chorale Inc., with Director Mary Abbott, Los Angeles, California

Neda Gray, Photographer, Westcoast California

Neil Thompson, Graphics Review and Moderator

Sister Phyllis Harris McDaniel Family

Dr. James Redden Family

George E. Whiting, Washington, DC

Henrietta White Family

LV Hawkins Family, Lake Providence, Louisiana

Lois Ferguson Family, Houston, Texas

Willie Mae Odom, Twin Sister to Lillie Mae Bailey

Marie, Odie, Linda, San, Rene, Bobbie, Margie, Kim, Aaron, -St Louis, Missouri

Myrtle Smith Veal Family with Bianchi Veal, Houston, Texas

Mayor Bobby and Sister Frances Washington, COGIC

Solomon and Family, Fort Washington, Maryland

Liynah, Ruth, Rachel, Rebekah – Washington, DC

The Peese Foundation for Yahweh

The Clara Howard Foundation, Minden, Louisiana

Sergeant Stewart and Colonel Smith, US Army

Authors Notes

Within reason, **prayers** are affective by language and often changed by dialect, religion, and beliefs. Each person has his own prayer and method of how a prayer can be spoken. The phenomena of this variable language and dialect is the least common denominator when we consider all that exist in the hemisphere of humanity. What and who would that phenomena be, characterized by nature and relative to prayer? This is the rhetorical question for all to seek and find in their given space.

A prayer spoken by 10,000 in multiple languages gathers the force of the wind on a stormy sea. Yet a prayer spoken by three in the same language on one accord can bring the stormy sea to calmness. Not our will but His will be done.

The collection of prayers gathered here was expressed in the home for more than 200 years. Invariably a select few prayers were contributed from friends of the family then included with our printed collection and research. Grand parents from a southern Christian background taught these family prayers to children and siblings shared the prayers in Christian communities. Out of these prayers are built Colonels, Judges, and Congressman to name the least.

As we write on the subject of prayer our intent is to encourage a new reader to action and motivate biblical study in everyday life. A hoped for systemic result of this writing is for you to direct your efforts to embrace God as the center for youth development and healthy activities. We are laymen, witnesses and servants who furthermore strive for excellence through harmony with God. Prayers in practice become a discipline, an order, and a sanctuary to your higher calling. This book is written to bear witness that God Is who He said He Is, The Great I AM, He delivers as promised and to share how we found Him in prayer. Bliss and Joy are waiting for you to seek your true purpose, then Master your gift with prayer. Bliss and Joy are introduced as if they are persons and you may well advance to think they are angelical beings, however, we specifically are referring to the experience of being Joy filled and in total Bliss where you are happy all the day without a particular event. This state of being is commonly known as 'peace of mind'; Do you know what Shalom is and do you have peace of mind? Did you have to think about this question or rationalize in any sense of the word?

There is a passage in Isaiah 49:8-9 – This is what the Lord says: In the time of my favor, I will answer you, and in the day of salvation I will help you; I will keep you and make you to be a covenant for the people, to restore the land and to reassign its desolate inheritances, to say to the captives 'Come out,' and to those in darkness, 'Be free!' These words given to the restoration of Israel are music to our ears; succinctly a repertoire of fine tuned breaths holding the power of life in a shear utterance. A long awaited call - that may have only been a day, while in that day a thousand years escaped us, now listen, 'Come out,' …....'Be free.'

Until I Learn To Pray implies a how to say collection of honest prayers spoken from our hearts. The words in their most simple form are shared with complete reverence to our God, The divine power within magnifies a need for you to understand and build your relationship with God. Refer to Zachariah 4:6 – Not by might, nor by power, but by my Spirit, says the Lord Almighty.

Background

In the early 1800's (1801-1807) our predecessors resided near the small town of Minden, Louisiana. The wooded region of their countryside abode was known as Blue Run. They were new people on a new land where adaptation and survival were key elements to our future. Amidst a rural development, all of their challenges had one saving grace – Prayer. Prayers were the music in the air, they were the morning greeting at sunrise, they were carefully stated with the appearance of a hot biscuit as chow. Prayers were repeated walking the long country miles to town and escalated to hallelujahs on the arrival home. The family Midwives shouted a prayer during a delivery at the birth of each child. And for the little ones, prayer was a knee bending exercise with an assurance of good health.

Each generation, for us, has a unified purpose – build our relationship with God: then expand a right dignity in respect of the interpersonal relationship with your fellow man. The fellow man is the family, the neighbor, the communities, the school staff, the workplace, the Church, the Temple, the Mosque, and the Synagogue. (*Conversation of Elder parent with daughter*) So, how could these prayers create or make such relationships among segmented faiths and authoritative entities as we have mentioned here? **The prayers were directed to the Sovereign One, as we extol Him, His will be done.** Were these persons of the 1800's doctors, or a Prophet, great men of wisdom? – **No.** Then in your teachings what was the lesson plan and can we utilize the same plan today? **The men taught their sons to fish and the women taught their daughters how to bake breads – Each was completed with prayer.**

That may have worked in the 1800's and early 1900's, however, these are modern times; the age of high technology, satellites, and moon ships. Is there a new plan? **If this was a song I would direct you to the first stanza...."Build your relationship with God, extol Him. God is the same yesterday, as today, and tomorrow." "Pray daily, yes, pray daily; teach your sons how to fish, teach your daughters how to bake, complete each activity with prayer." In other words when we teach our sons how to fish, we teach them all of the skills and God knowledge we have so they will eat for a lifetime. This also means they can provide a safe haven for their family. There are many lessons in the baking of breads that you can teach to your daughters.** The only lesson I readily associate with baking is you must have the right measures for each ingredient. **Consider in the activity of baking; there is a plan, a time to implement each stage of the plan, scientific measures of portions to yield substance for the number served, you must have the right temperature (*same as*** *right environment*), the baking rack level or altitude can impact your results, you must have patience as you mark time in the waiting, and always add a lot of love in the mix. Furthermore it is important to understand the characteristic of each ingredient; as you know some items can be substituted, however, not by the way they look. Parents can share with a child the raw ingredient has little or no resemblance to the finished product. Just as two new persons may enter a congregation of believers; one may enter wearing diamonds and gold while the other come with a plain penny-annie suit full of drama. How can they be transformed into leadership except to encounter Genesis to Revelation, line upon line and precept upon precept? God works with the inward parts while we only see the outer appearance.

Let us examine the significance of Yeast in the bread recipe. Yeast responds better when water is added then kept warm for the rise. The reaction in yeast gives off carbon dioxide as it is a living organism driven by its contact with sugar. The essence of a substance nature is a guide to how it reacts when compounded with others. The leavening action of yeast can be transferred and fermented from one batch of an older dough to another batch of a new dough having the same response, in a given time it will rise. Yeast is also known as organized ferment. All of these things are relative to life experiences; it is a benison, aiding you to make right decisions for the right purpose and season.

We as parents pray with our children while constantly sharing Truth. This is what must be included in our youth programs. In a 'spirituel' sense, God's word is Truth that act as a tumult in us, a living organism. Truth – the Testaments, Commandments, Scripture - God's instruction is to us as leaven is to bread. Prayer provides the warmth creating an environment for the Truth to ferment and rise in us at its proper time. When we send our children out in a world with no prayer such as public schools, teen activity centers, or youth programs - we remove the covering of warmth which is the protection that stabilizes and ensures their spiritual growth. Without the Truth and Prayer we are walking our children straightway to become empty vessels.

What was the purpose of the hand made quilts and why did you pray over them? The quilts allowed us to fellowship with one another while we sharpen our craft and practice several of Gods principles of the in-gathering. Explain this quilt- in-gathering- prayer-principle. Each person assisting with a quilt must share supplies such as threads, fabrics, patterns, a wood horse for framing, or baked goods. Upon entering the home where the quilting takes place, we conduct an inventory of available items – that is Mathematics having to measure the size quilt desired and count squares to form the full pattern. Following pattern layout is similar to bringing together different people from diverse cultures to participate in God's work in the Church or the Temple. Mothers with children can educate and teach each step of an activity to illuminate fundamental learning about God. We have to cut and shape all the pieces making them fit inside the top layer for the quilt. So, now you are saying each piece share an equal important part in forming the whole. Yes exactly. That is Sociology. We multiply the length of squares times the width of square to estimate the thread yardage required. That is Engineering. The blessing is we always seem to have just enough to finish as long as we do not waste. That is Economics. Never thought of quilting as being so important. Oh! more significant is after we have completed the quilt it is given to one family for their use. That is the spirit of Charity. When is the prayer spoken? We begin with a prayer and we end with a prayer. This strengthens our bond to be on one accord--- Also each time we turn the quilt we all pray that our work will complement the next persons craft and so on until it is finish.

Shall we enter into Prayer.......

HE, Jehovah, Yahweh, Father, Abba, Allah, GOD Almighty – Blessed is He -- does great things. This is a truth actualized by ones experience and relationship with The Sovereign Deity. More omnipotent than three hundred sixty degrees, one area we find God is in the volume of the Books. The most comprehensive book above all books ever written is the Holy Bible, instructions inspired of GOD. If you have not read and studied the Holy Bible, we recommend you do so immediately. How does a layman (average person) begin a relationship with God? Most start with an introduction similar to one given when in the presence of a stranger. A second person is present who is familiar with both you and the Infinite Light (when you are a stranger). The second person guides, collaborates, announces, and introduces you to a new acquaintance (when you are a stranger that somehow, at first, seems like an acquaintance of old). We view the familiarity of this acquaintance as The Light that shined into darkness; the same as when you exited the womb – God was there. Over time and through active interaction a relationship is built that lasts forever. A substantial gift is imparted each time you encounter The Sovereign One. Many encounters will yield a lesson, some an answer to your question, at times a healing is given, others a view into the future of where a path is directed. Yes, each time you ask of God, there is an answer --- Either Yes, or No, or Wait. As you read the contents of this book "Molahs Shalom Until I Learn to Pray", we look into the inner core of prayer. Do not stop with our research on prayer; ponder the words for yourself, place them on your heart, implement them in practice. You may travel light years beyond your current physical state into the realm of spiritual guidance.

Today, what is prayer? The word Prayer is a noun rooted in the word Pray -- a transitive verb, also known as précis. Pray is a means to implore by supplication. Précis is a concise abridgement or a summary. Let us open with light on the subject by saying we have a person-place-or thing; in this case prayer is a thing. The *thing* as prayer takes the form of its root transitive verb – when we pray; because now the thing is acted upon expressing existence. So to pray means to constitute existence. Return to précis which is the concise abridgement. To constitute a concise abridgement means we are working a concept of formula. Make a mental notation here that the process is *similar* to a formula, however not to be referred as, nor taken to be a formula in itself. The summary (*Précis or Pray*) is now *like* a method, a means, a frequency by which we entreaty God, recognize His existence in utterance and praise. In Greek, referenced because of its place in history, **proseuchomai** means pray with emphasis on directing our prayer to our Father.

It is your decision to move forward abound in elevation for life everlasting, a saving grace, as it is God's will. In Matthew 6:33 it is written "...Seek ye first the kingdom of God and his righteousness; and all these things shall be added unto you." As you read the prayers, repeat them. Learn to know a prayer for yourself and for your family. Exercise faith in all your work. Faith, the evidence of things hoped for, the substance of that not seen, is important because faith honors God and God honors faith. Remember Matthew 14:28-33. . . . .And Peter answered Him and said, Lord, if it be Thou, bid me come unto thee on the water. And he said COME. And when Peter was come down out of the ship, he walked on the water, to go to Jesus. But when he saw the wind boisterous, he was afraid; and beginning to sink, he cried, saying, Lord, save me.

And immediately Jesus stretched forth his hand and caught him, and said unto him, O thou of little faith, wherefore didst thou doubt?

And when they were come into the ship, the wind ceased. Then they that were in the ship came and worshiped Him, saying of a truth thou art the Son of God.

Jesus is so named for he shall save his people from their sins. The name Jesus Christ also means Savior and is referenced as Messiah by Christians. If there is one precept to understand here, see the connection of prayer with faith – you must know the Truth and the Truth shall set you free – believe when you pray, activate your faith to present a petition to the Messiah.

Jesus is said to have walked this planet over 2000 years ago, yet His teachings continue today as a model which guides us the way to live. Since the first coming of Christ many great men of Valor have brought the Message and may be thought of as a type of savior to those seeing the spirit of Truth in them or because of the masses of people positively affected by these Truth teachings. For some it is their Evangelist visited every Sunday; for many their messenger has been the highest Potentate of thought, for others it is an Imam, Monk, Rabbi, Priest or a Pope. How you receive the message of Christ teachings whether through visible contact, audible perception or the written word is an area of God Rulership above our knowledge as a layman, such as me. We humbly respect their position in history and their purpose for God they were so sent. Their presence reminds us that God still answers prayers.

This book is written for all people who believe in God and those who may come to know and believe in God. The text is directed to be written in a style that is simple and informative. A cross-cultural prefixed pronominal, in Greek it is said as "Ein", and in English we say "The One" as a common thread not to limit you to religion and rituals. Our prayer now is that today you will be prompted to take hold of life with children of your area, introduce them to God, be a vessel for their development. For those who have yet to know God and believe in God, this book may serve as a witness and a tool which, "God willing", places understanding to enhance a spiritual building where in journey He may draw you nearer to the Sovereign One.

Molahs Shalom (*A Return To Peace*) is named for the peace inside of Shalom. The word Molahs was created for this book in an effort to accompany your awakening of cognitive senses toward a pinnacle for higher learning. Shalom is a greeting from the Hebrew meaning

"I come in peace". Where the word Salaam is found – this is the Arabic writing of Shalom having the same meaning of peace. "**Until I Learn to Pray**", God gives me peace ever lasting. Each return to Him is the Molahs[1], in honor of His divine sacred order, He is the Shalom. When Molahs Shalom (*when you return to* God) are combined they form a circle of energy, a life force that prompts the memory to submission in mercy to God's will.

Molahs Shalom

---

1   Molahs is a right to left reading of Shalom. Meant only to replicate English shalom.. Implicates a return to God. No other meaning should be applied for world languages.

Forward

Prayer is a conversation with God. Most often known as what we engage ourselves with daily is our prayer. Let us begin with the 66 word prayer taught to the Disciples of Christ (can be found in the book of Matthew 6 Chapter 9-13 verses). [Mat 6:9-13]

The Lord's Prayer

Our Father which art in heaven,
Hallowed be Thy name.
Thy kingdom come
Thy will be done
On earth as it is in heaven.
Give us this day our daily bread
Forgive us our debts,
As we forgive our debtors.
And lead us not in to temptation,
But deliver us from evil.
For thine is the kingdom, and the power
And the glory, for ever. Amen.

Consider when these 66 words are spoken, and if allowed to be mathematically expressed as 6+6=12. (12 is 1+2)=3. Three is our universal Trinity. Now further consider God exist in, as a part of the Trinity and beyond – for He is everywhere. The prayer is spoken to the One God, likewise, 3 is now added to the One God and there is 4 (four represents foundation) – a foundation by which lives are built. To our dear Elders as you read this passage, understand why it is written. Imagine being in a world where prayer is rarely heard. Prayer was removed from the schools, removed from meal-time (thus our daily bread), and scattered – almost not there in the homes. What if all you know is basic math such as what is written *like* a formula of 3 + 1 = 4 and that four represents a square and a square forms the foundation of a building. What are we remembering?   --The Chief Cornerstone must be the "Ein" , The One, to build lives. Humbly in gratitude – dear Elders we thank you. A major point to apprehend clearly in the Mathematics of learning is stay on course, base each letter as a blueprint to the Word. Consider what was read from the beginning is you may build a first or better relationship with God. This relationship is brought into existence when you acknowledge Him and strengthened by a continuous interaction. Your reading of his instructions and remembering God in all that you do: He is First, He is a part of your everyday life, and He is the purpose of your decisions.

We are sharing MIRACLES today that were experienced by our family in many instances which may reside only in the subconscious left side of our brain. When we maneuver through life with overlooked blessings we have cause to pray a prayer of forgiveness for the seen and the unseen, forgive us for our secret faults.

MIRACLE A

Prayer is a privilege we have of conversing intimately with God. We can beckon Him into our lives daily by simply ask in prayer (conversation). Pray boldly with confidence that your prayers be answered." The effectual fervent prayer of a righteous man availeth much." [James 5:16]. Remember God responds to our request out of Love. Ask, and it will be given you. Seek, and you will find: Knock, and the door will be opened to you. [Luke 11:9]

The Lord's Prayer interpreted by Reverend Doctor Hugh MacMillan, DD, LLD, FRSE, presents a master summary for practical application. He states The Lord's Prayer is the true model of prayer –"After this manner," "When we pray, say" etc. It lays down the lines on which we should frame our petitions; removes the distance and ceremoniousness of our approach to God; counteracts the selfishness of our desires; and enlarges our horizon so as to comprehend the welfare of the whole world. It was given by Christ to his disciples on two different occasions; the first in connection with the Sermon on the Mount; the second after two years, when the disciples asked Jesus to teach them how to pray. It is the Ten Commandments turned into prayer, the commandments to keep God's law being converted into prayers to enable us to keep that law. There is a striking correspondence between each clause of the Lord's Prayer and one of the commandments, and the order in which they mutually occur.

It consists, first, of an invocation or mode of address to God. The word "Our" indicates the great change which Christ introduced into the whole conception of worship. The worship of God is for all the people, with one heart and one voice.

Our 'Father". The relationship of God as a Father belongs to all men alike by right of creation and providence: it is by the grace of God in conversation that we receive the spirit of adoption, whereby we cry, "Abba, Father".

The words *"which art in heaven"* imply that as our Father is in heaven, so our desires and affections should ascend beyond earth.

The order of the petitions is very remarkable. It begins with the recognition of God's rights as Maker, Sovereign, Proprietor—"Thy name," Thy kingdom," "Thy will"; and then it goes on to the recognition of man's needs—our bread, our debts, our temptations, and our deliverance. The essence of sin is the inversion of this divine order, putting the creature first and the Creator last, giving precedence to man's need over God's rights.

"*Hallowed be thy name*" teach us that as children we are to treat with a holy love and fear the name and relation of Father in which we stand to God.

"*Thy kingdom come*" is a petition that God's reign of righteousness and peace and joy may be set up in our hearts, and that we may be enabled to extend it by our character, conduct, and work in the world.

"*Thy will be done in earth, as it is in heaven*" shows to us that God's will is the highest ultimate good of all his creatures; that all his laws have been devised to bring about this result; and that in proportion as we obey this will is our true welfare promoted. When our will and the Father's are absolutely one, we shall know that all things work together for our good.

"*Give us this day our daily bread*" At first sight referring to the most urgent want of man, we find that this petition is only one out of several others: not the first as the most important, not the last as the longest remembered, but enclosed among those which refer to spiritual things, to the establishment of God's kingdom and the overthrow of satan's. If we hallow God's name and submit to his reign and seek to do His will, then we can with confidence ask Him for the blessings which our natural life requires for its support and welfare. God gives us that for which we ourselves have to toil; not arbitrarily, but by wise and beneficent law; not all at once, but day by day.

"Forgive us our debts, as we forgive our debtors." The word "forgive"," being made up of the preposition "from," means literally "allow our debts to be put away from us." The word "debt" has a very close resemblance to the word "duty"; and our debts are therefore our failures in duty. We ask God to take away from us the carelessness and indifference in which such failures originate; not to save us from our obligations or the consequences of our sin, but from our sin itself. Forgive us not in proportion as, but like as, we forgive others. If we forgive others slowly, grudgingly, coldly, so shall we be treated.

"And lead us not into temptation." It is by temptation that we are tried and educated; yet we are justified in praying to our Father not to lead us into temptation so long as we leave with childlike submission, to his loving will, the means by which our faith is to be strengthened and our spiritual life purified and ennobled. We are not to go willingly into temptation. The temptation itself is not sin, but we fear that we may sin through it. Therefore, this petition is linked along with the next, so as to make of the two one petition. *"Deliver us from evil."* Knowing God's power we ask him to deliver us from the evil that is in the temptation, relying upon his promise that he will not suffer us to be tried above what we are able, but with every temptation will provide a way of escape.

"For thine is the kingdom, and the power, and the glory, for ever" may be considered a

doxology. It is an appropriate ending of the Lord's Prayer, giving us good grounds of encouragement to pray, and at the same time ascribing all the praise to God. It is for His glory that all worship is carried on, therefore He will hear our prayer, and do for us exceeding abundantly above all that we can ask or think. "Amen"

In your learning, understand that prayer is not a technique; however, it is a bold and persistent way we respond to God's grace. After prayers, Repent: change the course of direction of your life to righteous living and fulfill the purpose as called by God.

You may ask "What is the significance of the body form when we enter into prayer?" Many bow their heads, some close the eyes, other body forms have expression with hands stretched forth lowered or raised. Some kneel and some flatten the entire body in a limbs spread toward the earth and symbolic practices may face the sun.

- Heads bowed in prayer represent humble submission to God.
- Eyes closed in prayer imply exclusion from the world and centering the Holy Spirit.
- Hands raised with all fingers straight upward, open palms, facing the east denotes a surrender, all of me, to God. Reference to a Sunrise (The Son) in the east, in the last days turn toward (The Son) rise in the west.
- Hands stretched forth clasped together with fingers pointed upward is directing earthly energy from the body toward a heavenly encounter.
- Hands lowered met at the miniature fingers (minimus) as to form a bowl. Palms open upward implies belief the prayer will be answered and the requester is positioned to receive the blessing.
- Hands clasped together with fingers overlap to back of each hand represents union in meekness.
- Kneeling in prayer with one or both knees bent to the floor or bench surface denotes a humble sincerity to be transmitted.
- Body flatten and spread has relation to the Sephiroth (ten attributes of transfiguration), totality of the meek in spirit. All yielding to heavenly beings— God, His Angels, the Holy Throne.
- Sit upright with legs crossed, hands resting on knees. A vertical //horizontal connection with the universe to zone the senses.

Great is our Lord, and of great power: His understanding is infinite. Knowledge of God allows you to pray with all body forms previously stated or standing, sitting, or at rest. In other words wherever you are and however positioned, you can pray. Always pray with reverence to God. In Matthew 6:6 it is written "…when thou prayest, enter into thy closet, and when thou hast shut thy door, pray to thy Father which is in secret…".

We pray for ourselves, a soul salvation or healing. We pray to strengthen our relationship with God, and to uphold unity with our fellow man. These prayers may lead to unlimited conversations with God extending the conscious request from Alpha to Omega or from A to Z. When prayers are given for another, for a special purpose in a defined circumstance it is called Intercessory Prayer. Know when we touch and agree there is power in our prayer. Such as a prayer by a father for his son, a mother for her children, a sister for her brother, a wife for her husband, a team with a minister for one player, may be considered intercessory prayers. Yet, His will be done.

MIRACLE B

Water

The living waters of truth have been said to satisfy the soul. We can speak on endless healing needs for the body and for mans soul. The fact of the matter is an ill body or an ill soul will hunger and thirst for an unknown quencher to balance and align a seemingly mistuned instrument -- the body. Natural Water is a compound made of two parts hydrogen and one part oxygen. Scientist confirmed the symbol for oxygen is 'O' (full circle as Omnipotent). Scientist further confirmed the atomic number of oxygen is 8 (in universal math 8 is new beginning). We breathe in oxygen and exhale or breathe out carbon dioxide. The relationship of man to plants as we know it is plants release oxygen and take in carbon dioxide (our daily bread). A connection repeats throughout every documented scroll, each breath of life is a new beginning. The restless effect of an ill physical state sends constant signals to the soul for emergency rescue. In a collapsed condition of the soul, meaning there is no oxygen – a required element for life, makes the soul unresponsive to the very essence of its existence. Just as water seeks it's level, here we found the body yearns to fill a void with the Omnipotent, or to us, God. Furthermore, even a resourceful entity may need assistance to find how to store oxygen in the soul which when combined with the hydrogen of life – released as we speak scripture, will lead them to the living waters of truth (Absolute Truth), a healing.

Those who are restless and dissatisfied with themselves and their life are in craving for something more. They need a greater understanding of their place in life. They need spiritual truth. The God inside is calling them to come up higher. We must open our mind and life to spiritual truth as we find God in our midst. In John 4:14 reads "Whosoever drinks of the water that I shall give him will never thirst; the water that I shall give him will become in him a spring of water welling up to eternal life."[2]

A natural process in life is growth. Just as a seed sprouts when water is poured on the soil where the seed is planted, so will your life be when living waters of truth sprinkle your mind. This growth is synonymous with change. Yes, expect a change in your life for the better when you pray.

---

[2] Daily Word - May 1982

Let us return to the word PRAYER in relationship to growth and change. The original Hebrew word for prayer is referred as *tefillah*. The *tefillah* may be considered sealed in the hearts of many just as Solomon likened God's revelation to a seal. [3] When one stamps something with a seal, it produces a mirror image. The growth and change that takes place within us is a divine visualizing of what is sealed in our hearts. Likewise, Molahs is a return to the mirror image of Shalom. A persistent motion toward God is a means of prayer through which we work under His guidance, that we are walking in God's light, expressing God's love. We then have the assurance that all things are working together for the good. Yet, His will be done.

---

3   Rabbi M. Munk

MIRACLE C

By now you may have given thought to a prayer that you have prayed. When you pray allow a spiritual transition in words while you focus on God and consider the activity of your prayer. For example; if you pray to present yourself a worthy believer to hold an office in a Temple – you may change by turning to God with trust, being more responsible in daily work and preparing for each Sabbath Day lesson before each Sabbath Day is met. Prayer validated with submission to His Will opens the door to making your action parallel your voice so as to step toward God. Return to Him and He will return to you. *MIRACLE C* often occurs in perpetual motion. Read the prayers as if you are entering a field of harvest that meets all of your needs. Carry a basket with you to hold the items that you recognize as an answer to your call, to be gathered for safe keeping. If you fall along the way, get up and continue moving in a forward direction, remember perpetual motion. You may meet many persons in the field of harvest. As they approach you some will nod their heads down with chin to chest then an upward motion toward the sky – they are sharing with you "Jesus Saves"; smile and continue moving forward. When you are on the right path others will greet you with a smile so that you know it is well, it is well, it is well. If the basket becomes too heavy with the harvest that meets your needs, give it to God , you can always find it there. If it is your heart's desire to complete this journey there may be requirements of you to be dexterous or circumspect. The field is huge which means it can take more than one day to complete while the sun sets and darkness shadows the land, you must be incandescent. During the dark season, hold closer to the Comforter (God's Word). This will rebuke those attempting to have you turn back. Remember your previous lessons if you thirst, MIRACLE B can digest as a roborant to assist and energize on this path. If a tiredness overwhelm you that causes you to look back; You will see Grace and Mercy as they are always behind you—remember how far you have come. Take His yoke (Jesus) upon you. His yoke is easy and the burden is light. You will know as you approach the exit for the pathway is straight and narrow. Again focus on the inestimable attributes of God, there are at least 99 attributes of God to comfort you throughout this journey. Pray for His Name sake. Yet, His will be done.

Morning Sunrise Prayers

Prayer 2

Our heavenly Father, God
Thank you for this day
May my steps be made for your purpose
Thank you for a peaceful night rest. Amen.

Prayer 3

Father of Glory
All power is in your hands
I give myself to thee
Use me as you will that Thy will be done. Amen, amen, amen.

Prayer 4

Our Father, Master of All,
God of our forefathers Abraham, Isaac, and Jacob
Bring a perfect peace into our lives today.
Fix me, bless us as a family, and strengthen our bond

Oh Holy One of Israel, Yahweh
Keep us safe. Amen

Prayer 5

God, the Omnipotent
Shine your light in our lives today
Help us to see you clearer
Guide us to a better place
Let our minds be blessed with understanding
Allow our hearts to be filled with love
May we bring a smile to ones you choose
And Joy to a needed person
Grant us abilities to share mercy. Amen

Prayer 6

Our Father we approach the Throne of Grace
Open our minds, open our hearts, open our eyes
To see you as you will
Humbly we pray for a blessed day.
Lift us up where we have fallen
Increase courage in us to affirm decisions
Strengthen us where we are weak
Plant our feet on solid ground.
We trust you, We believe in Christ—that
He died for our sins and rose again that we may have
A right to the tree of life. We claim our right to the tree of life.
These blessings we ask in your Son Jesus name, Amen.

Prayer 7

Father, Father, Father
Come into my life today
Make straight the crooked
Make wise my simple thoughts
Make humble my offerings to you
Allow a meekness in my attitude and
A reasonable service in my actions.
Forgive our transgressions, allow us to correct our errors and Father send help to correct our mistakes. Amen.

Prayer 8

Father of the Universe
Creator of all that exist in our lives, You are the
Author and Finisher of my soul
Grant us this day a spirit of thankfulness
Multiply our vision to see your great works
Build within us a line and a precept to your glorious kingdom
We honor you Father, we thank you Father
Allow us to reach one lost soul today that
Yearns for your love.
Guide us on the journey of righteousness
Bless the Lord, Oh my soul. Amen

Divine Guidance

Prayer 9

Our Father
Thank you for our lives, thank you for our children
Thank you for our sisters and brothers, our mom and dad
Thank you for the church family, thank you for our teachers and ministers of your word.
Thank you for the stranger who is obedient to your word. Thank you for the prophets,
the disciples and the ambassadors of Christ. Thank you for the covenant
Thank you for discernment, righteous judgement, and your love
Keep us in Thy will dear Father
In Jesus name we pray, Amen, amen and amen.

Prayer 10

The Lord is my shepherd
I shall not want
He maketh me to lie down in green pastures
He leadeth me beside the still waters
He restoreth my soul
He leadeth me in the path of righteousness
For His name sake
Yeah though I walk through the valley
Of the shadow of death
I will fear no evil, for thou art with me
Thy rod and thy staff they comfort me
Thou preparedest a table before me in the presence of mine enemies
Thou anointest my head with oil
My cup runneth over
Surely goodness and mercy shall follow me all the days of my life
And I will dwell in the house of the Lord forever. Amen   [*Psalms 23*]

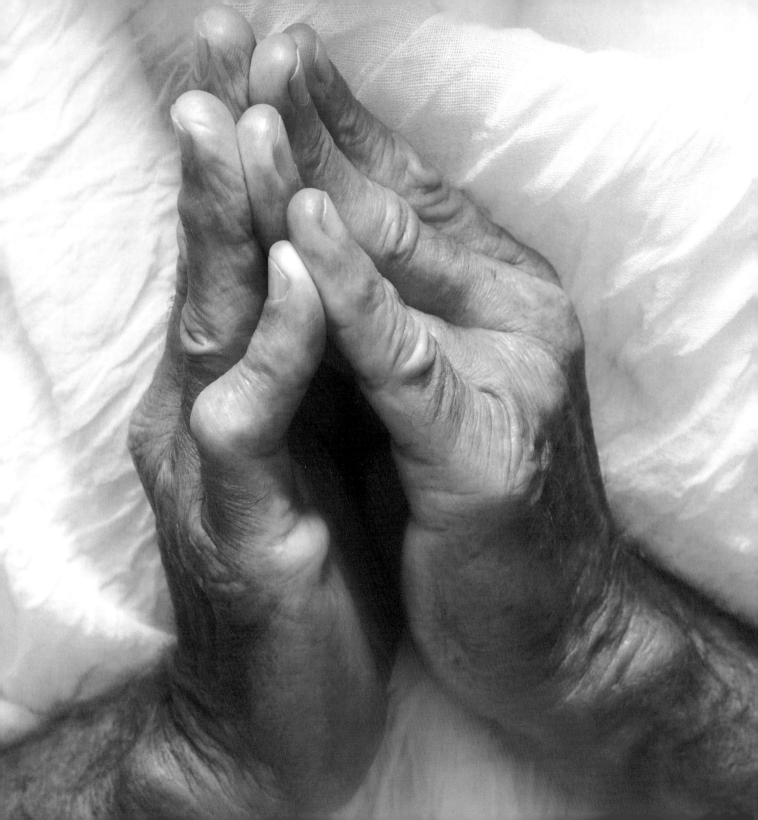

Prayer 11

Lord, make me an instrument of Thy peace;
Where there is hatred, let me sow love;
Where there is injury, pardon;
Where there is doubt, faith;
Where there is despair, hope;
Where there is darkness, light;
And where there is sadness, joy. Amen.   [*St Francis Assisi*]

Prayer 12

God, Our Father
Grant us the courage to respond to hate with love
So that we may reflect your mercy
And help your love prevail
In Jesus name we pray. Amen[4]

Prayer 13

Dear Lord
Provide me with a few friends who understand me
And yet remain my friends
A work to serve in a duty which has real value
Without which the world would feel the void
A mind unafraid to travel even though the trail is not blazed
An understanding heart, a sense of humor
Time for quiet, silent meditation

---

[4]   Adult Bible Studies, United Metheodist Publishing House(2007 by Cokesbury)

A feeling of your presence, God
And the patience to wait for the coming of these things
With the wisdom to know them when they are here. Amen

Prayer 14

Gracious God
Help us hear Jesus call to discipleship. Grant us strength
And understanding to respond positively
With every fiber of our being
Sustain and strengthen us each day as we serve you.
In Jesus name we pray. Amen[5]

Prayer 15

Father of Love and mercy
Grant us this day a closer walk with thee.
Open a door that was closed
Lift us higher to see you Dear God
Allow your will be done in my life today
For righteous purification, holy deliverance, and justified faith
We praise your holy name. Amen.

---

5   Adult Bible Studies, United Methodist Publishing House(2007 Cokesbury)

Prayer 16

Our Father

Have mercy upon me, O God, according to thy loving-kindness:

According unto the multitude of thy tender mercies

Blot out my transgressions

Wash me thoroughly from mine iniquity, and cleanse me from my sin

For I acknowledge my transgressions; and my sin is ever before me

Against thee, thee only, have I sinned and done this evil in thy sight:

That thou mightest be justified when thou speakest and be clear when thou judgest.

Behold, I was shapen in iniquity; and in sin did my mother conceive me.

Behold, thou desirest truth in the inward parts; and in the hidden part thou shalt make me to know wisdom.

Purge me with hyssop, and I shall be clean; wash me and I shall be whiter than snow.

Amen.   [*Psalm 51:1-7*]

Midday Prayers

Prayer 17

Father God
Jesus wept and bless the Lord Oh my soul
Bless this food, may it be utilized for the nourishment of our bodies
For Christ sake, our strength and our redeemer
These and many blessings we ask in Jesus name. Amen.

Prayer 18

Our Father
We bow in your presence
Strengthen our feet that we not stumble
Help us to see your light in those we meet
Allow our ears to hear a word from you
As we listen unknowingly to voices sent by you
Grant us peace that we will share peace with everyone met today
Forgive our sins of omission and commission,
Empower us with your righteous will

Multiply our deeds of good will and make a place in your kingdom for our children,
Protect us in the seen and the unseen
Help us to teach our children the straight and narrow way of life,
That we raise them up to follow the teachings of Christ, believe in you God, respect, honor and praise God even give the same respect and honor to our fellow man. Place in our children the Golden Rule – Do unto others as you would have them do unto you.
Knowing you are our one and only true and living God,
We bless your holy name.   Amen.

Prayer 19

Father of Glory
We come to you asking that you will speak through us
As we stand on your principles
We ask you not limit us to our thoughts but expound in us a word from you,
When we engage in battle, protect us with the holy grail, the coat of armour, the full breast plate of God. Help us to know the battle is not ours and we give it to you.
Move us at God speed before the Throne of Grace, let us be made in your image
Bring a Pentecostal experience as we unite and support one love to another. Induce a labor of new ideas sent from heaven,
Give us birth to the demonstration of your New Testament
Allow our children to authenticate what was formed from the foundation of the earth, before "In the beginning," recognize you are the great I AM.
These and many blessings we ask in Jesus name. Amen.

Prayer 20

Master, our Savior
You are worthy, our Lord and God
To receive glory and honor and power, for you created all things
And by your will they were created and have their being. Amen.

Prayer 21

Our Father,
Lover of my soul
Worthy is the Lamb of God
Amen.

Prayer 22

Dear God,
It is You and me, and I praise you Father,
I lift you up
Order my steps in your word as I stand in the need of prayer
I love you Father
Bless you forever and ever. Amen.

Prayer 23

Heavenly Father,
Thank you for saving us, sanctifying us and washing us in the blood of your Son. I look at my hands and they look new. I look at my feet and new they are too.
My walk is changed
My talk is about you Heavenly Father, and the building of your kingdom
We are singing a new song
Thank you Father, thank you. Amen.

Prayer 24

God of Grace
Bless the children of our community
Help us teach them your righteous ways, the Ten Commandments, the Pentateuch Law and good judgment,
Make us a positive example for others to follow. Show them through our collective efforts how to take up the cross and follow Jesus.
Make clear the vision of your yoke, For it is easy and the burden is light
Give the children a clean heart to follow you. Amen.

Prayer 25

Dear Father God,
Dwell among us in our daily walk
Guide us to higher heights with wisdom and understanding
We love you Father. Amen.

Prayer 26

Barouch Hashem
Selah

Prayer 27

Our Father
All things are possible through Christ whom we love
Amen.

Prayer 28

Father God,
We cast our bread upon the waters
We submit to your word for courage and guidance
We believe and have faith in all the testaments
We believe all that the Prophets have told us
We believe in the Holy Spirit, that Jesus died and rose again for our sins,
That we may have a right to the tree of life. Amen

Prayer 29

Father God
Walk with me Lord
Talk with me Lord
Guide me to your holy place. Amen.

Prayer 30

God of mercy, God of grace,
Bless our children, let their face be always turned to you O'Lord
Open their ears to hear, their eyes to see,
Allow them to come on bending knees
Ready to receive your direction
Lead them to do thy will
Humbly we pray. Amen.

Prayer 31

Our Sovereign Father
Your love is all we need and
All power is in your hand
Let our thoughts be pure and
Let our hearts be made clean to serve you in the kingdom of righteousness
We honor you God, we worship you
Praise be to the Father forever. Amen

Prayer 32

Father, Father, Father
My friend TA is in need of your love, grace, and mercy dear God
We stand as intercession to assist that which you provide—his needs and concerns, Father
Guide him with your light. Make him strong to lead in safety and spiritual magnitudes according to your riches.
Let his walk exemplify your holiness
May Christ life be paralleled in his abilities to teach and serve you Father.
Amen.

Prayer 33

Our Father,

…Oh that thou wouldest bless me indeed, and enlarge my coast, and that thine hand might be with me, and that thou wouldest keep me from evil,

That it may not grieve me. Amen. [1 Chronicles 4:10] *(Prayer of Jabez)*

Prayer 34

Father God,

We love you

We humbly submit ourselves to you that thy will be done in our lives

Lead us to our purpose.

Keep us contributing always to the purpose you set for our life

Send a special blessing to our Sunday School Class 7A

Bless each and everyone that attends the Sunday School

Unite us according to your will

Place in us leadership to teach others your word

This we ask in Christ Jesus name

Amen.

Prayer 35

Master of the Universe

We come before you in a prayer of building

Of the Tabernacle

Understanding dear God, that which is bind on earth shall be bound in heaven and whatsoever ye shall loose on earth shall be loosed in heaven

Remembering dear God, we are given the chief corner stone to set the foundation of our building

Believing dear God, that the true Tabernacle was made within us placed in plan from the Genesis of life

We pray the cultivation and yielding of our first fruits be a pure reflection

Of your glory.

Magnify our faith to build a holy consecrated structure of worship in accord to your will. May our tabernacle of faith be a harbor of love, learning, protection, spiritual development, and truth under your divine peace and provisions. In this Tabernacle may the ambiance of your light be a beacon for the lost soul to find their way to you dear God.

Make every brick of this new building represent a principle of faith. Establish a sacred love among our congregation; have us on one accord, with all things in common.

When this is all said and done dear God

Let each one teach one.

This and many blessings we ask in thy son Jesus name. Amen.

Prayer 36

God Jehovah
I pray for a word from you this day
Thank you Father for time until time is no more
Amen

Prayer 37

God Yahweh
You are my All in All
We bless your holy name.
Amen.

Prayer 38

Jehovah Jirah
You are my provider
Thank you for Father Solomon in the niche of time
I pray for a hedge of protection be placed around the Nation
Guard our children, keep their minds clean,
Their hearts pure, their bodies healthy,
That they grow up to be strong , yet wise soldiers in the army of God
Amen.

Prayer 39

Father of Mercy
Bless my sisters and brothers, whom I love.
Amen

Prayer 40

Father God
Make my life to do thy will; Make me a positive servant to the abilities given by you
Let each work give honor to you dear God for your name sake
Allow the reader of this prayer receive a message from you God
Allow the receiver of the message move closer toward you and respond to your will.
Allow the responder to your will be consciously bless with a renewed mind and spirit, and much to the giving of love one to another.
Make these blessings pressed down, shaken up and running over.
This we ask in thy son's name. Amen.

Prayer 41

Father Jehovah,

For I am not ashamed of the gospel of Christ; For it is the power of God unto salvation to every one that believeth:

The just shall live by faith

Understanding all have sinned and come short of the glory of God.

Being justified freely by his grace through redemption that is in Christ Jesus

Understanding "whom God hath set forth to be a propitiation through faith in his blood, to declare his righteousness for the remission of sins that are past, through the forbearance of God." [*Romans 1-3*]

We declare and pray for these in our life,

Amen.

Mealtime Prayer

Prayer 42

Our Father,
God is great
God is good
Lord we thank you for this food
Amen.

Prayer 43

Our Father
Thank you for this blessed meal
Bless the cook, bless the family for hosting our presence
These and many blessing we ask in thy son Jesus name. Amen.

End of the Day

Prayer 44

Our Abba
Lord lay me down to sleep
I pray the Lord my soul to keep
If I die before I wake
I pray the Lord my soul to take
Bless Moma, bless Daddy, bless sister, bless brother.
Amen.

Prayer 45

Master of All
We can do all things through Christ
Guide us through all activity done in righteousness
Lead us to make right, good, pertinent decisions in truth
Reveal to us false witnesses
Strengthen us in faith, in mind, in action
All power is in your hand.
We yield under control to your power.
Thank you for all the help you provided through the ages and
Thank you for a future in your love evermore. Amen.

Prayer 46

Master of All,
We love you. Fill our minds with wisdom
Incline our hearts to understanding
Amen.

Prayer 47

Master of All
Position us to serve you
Move us to unified efforts
Elevate our results to success.
Amen

Prayer 48

Father, Father, Father
Make a strong network of actions in my life
For the sake of your name
Thy will be done
Multiply your blessings. Bless us to bless others.
Amen.

Prayer 49

Father God
Open the eyes of our brothers
Make them leaders
Make them honest
Save them strong

Lift them high
Empower your purpose in them
Forever. Amen.

Prayer 50

Father, Master of the Universe
Teach us to number our days
That we apply our hearts to wisdom
Incline our visions to spark an everlasting flame of light
To empower truth over filander, distrust, and deceit.
Make us a permanent interest in thy love.
Make a compass of your instruction
Build a tower to the heaven promised
With bellowing support to those less fortunate
Than we are in this day.
Sprinkle laughter in our hearts
Spread a rainbow ribbon to connect
Us in honest service to the building
Of the Royal Tabernacle
May the structure begin with You Father, as you are within us and amplify an illumination
Toward God conscious thoughts and actions.
These and many blessings to our home
We ask for your righteous will.
Amen.

A Prayer For The Nation
To Our Father

Navigate a rulership for harmony, humble, straight and narrow perception that extricates freshly saturated boards, groups, and domiciles.

Alter a predestined destructive policy made in selfish latitude to appease a segregated monopoly hidden in a barrage of gifts to five percent of a starving country.

Transform mechanical apparatuses cloaked as human into a natural community. Make the new world leaders liken unto the New Testament with grace and honor, God willing.

Irrigate the halls of Congress with the living waters of truth. Make the least resistant House spring forth a fountain from which all may drink to the health of our nation.

Overturn overtime an architecture of a nation constructed to the blue print of a fundamentally sound plan – to reveal your plan. Set the axis for evolution among our administration to mathematics, to change only by a spiritual quotient manifested in real numbers for the betterment of the least of yours.

Now we yield to your will… In the name of Christ, Amen.

Prayer 51

Our Father
Bless all our members in this message;
May the God who gives endurance
And encouragement give you a spirit of unity among yourselves as you Follow Christ
teachings, so that with one heart and mouth you may glorify the God and Father of our
Lord Jesus Christ. Amen. [Romans 15:5-6]

Prayer 52

Father God
Keep us as salt with good savor
Protect us from apostacy
Let our yield be not of the fig tree in a storm
Allow us to serve you with first fruits
Peace be unto our house. Amen

Prayer 53

O Lord God
We adore you as being in control of everything
Riches and honor come from you alone.
It is at your discretion that men are made great and given strength.
O' our God, we thank you and praise your glorious name
But who am I and who are my people that we should be permitted to give anything to
you? Everything we have has come from you,
And we only give you what is yours already,
It all belongs to you. Amen [1 Chron 29:10-16]

Prayer 54

Bless the Lord O' my soul.
We lift up your holy name, Yahweh, in prayer.
Consecrate us and make us whole again unto yourself.
Thank you dear Father for waking us up
This morning clothe in our right mind,
Having good health and strength
You laid us down dear Father with grace
so that our bed was not our cooling board
and our sheet was not the winding sheet
You have brought us through from unconscious to conscious reality.
Given us the spirit of truth. Your angels laid poultice on our body for a healing. You
have raised us from the valley of dry bones,
Connected the sinews and given the breath of life
You have shown us the wheel in the middle of the wheel We thank you God.
Amen.

Prayer 55

Father, Heavenly Father
I will bless the Lord at all times
Praise will continuously proceed out of my mouth
Amen.

Prayer 56

Our Father
I trust the God spirit within
I turn away from external thoughts and look to the spirit within
As Jesus said "Come ye yourselves apart into a desert place, and rest a while." [*St Mark 6:31*]
I also come praying for us all.
Amen

Prayer 57

Dear Father, God of yesterday, today, and tomorrow
Your love is in my heart. Help me to see the good, the purpose of encounter, and a significance of how to fulfill your will in the people I meet.
Make in me a peace to share with the world whom you choose.
Bring a balance in my life and help me to walk always with your light.
Nurture your ideas in me, a vision to utilize in living a worthy, prosperous, fulfilling, life. Bring the vision to fruition with God speed, as thy will be done. This I ask in your son Jesus name, Amen.

Prayer 58

God Almighty,
Increase in me: "the fruit of the spirit is love, joy, peace, patience, kindness, goodness, faithfulness, gentleness, self-control;" [Galatians 5:22]
Amen.

Prayer 59

Our Father,
God, you are the highest,
I reverence thee.
"Thou dost keep him in perfect peace,
Whose mind is stayed on thee,
Because he trusts in thee." [Isaiah 26:3]
I love you. Amen.

Prayer 60

Our Father,
God, most praised, most loved, Omnipotent One.
"Heal me, O Lord, and I shall be healed;
Save me, and I shall be saved;
For thou art my praise." [Jeremiah 17:14]
Amen.

Prayer 61

Our Father,
Most High God,
We worship thee in spirit and truth.
Thank you for your ever lasting mercies and
Thank you for the serene power of your grace.
Quicken our spirits to reverence the redeeming love
In righteous obedience to your will.
Increase a sharing of truths in our homes and
Make that sharing throughout our communities.
Elevate our thinking to lead in righteousness
Raise the bar in our state to meet a new generation of
Believers in your word, dear Father, most high God.
As miracles were made in the beginning of time,
Set from the foundation of the carth,
As a robin was made to sing,
And a sparrow watched over the land, allow us to see your miracles today.
Your infinite wisdom existed before understanding and continues eternally.
Thank you.
Knowing the supple tenderness of a rain drop in the summer fields,
Makes our nourishment throughout winter – we worship thee.
Thank you, Most High God.
Thank you in spirit and in truth.
For your mercies and grace we are ever grateful.
Amen and amen.

Prayer 62

Our Father
Sanctify your word in me through truth
Your word is truth
I believe on your word
Amen.

Prayer 63

Our Father, Most High God,
I believe: "the kingdom of heaven is like unto treasure hid in a field;
That which when a man hath found, he hideth, and for joy thereof and sell all that he hath, and buy that field."
Again I believe: "the kingdom of heaven is like unto a merchant man, seeking goodly pearls; who when he had found one pearl of great price,
Went and sold all that he had and bought it."
I pray my life be a parable of praise to you.
Amen.

Prayer 64

Father God,
Liken unto me a wise man
That I build my house upon a rock
Understanding dear Father,
I build on the teachings of Christ.
Teach me to build a spiritual home
May I patiently chisel and shape virtue, humility, perseverance and love of God.
This blessing I ask in the name of Christ Jesus. Amen.

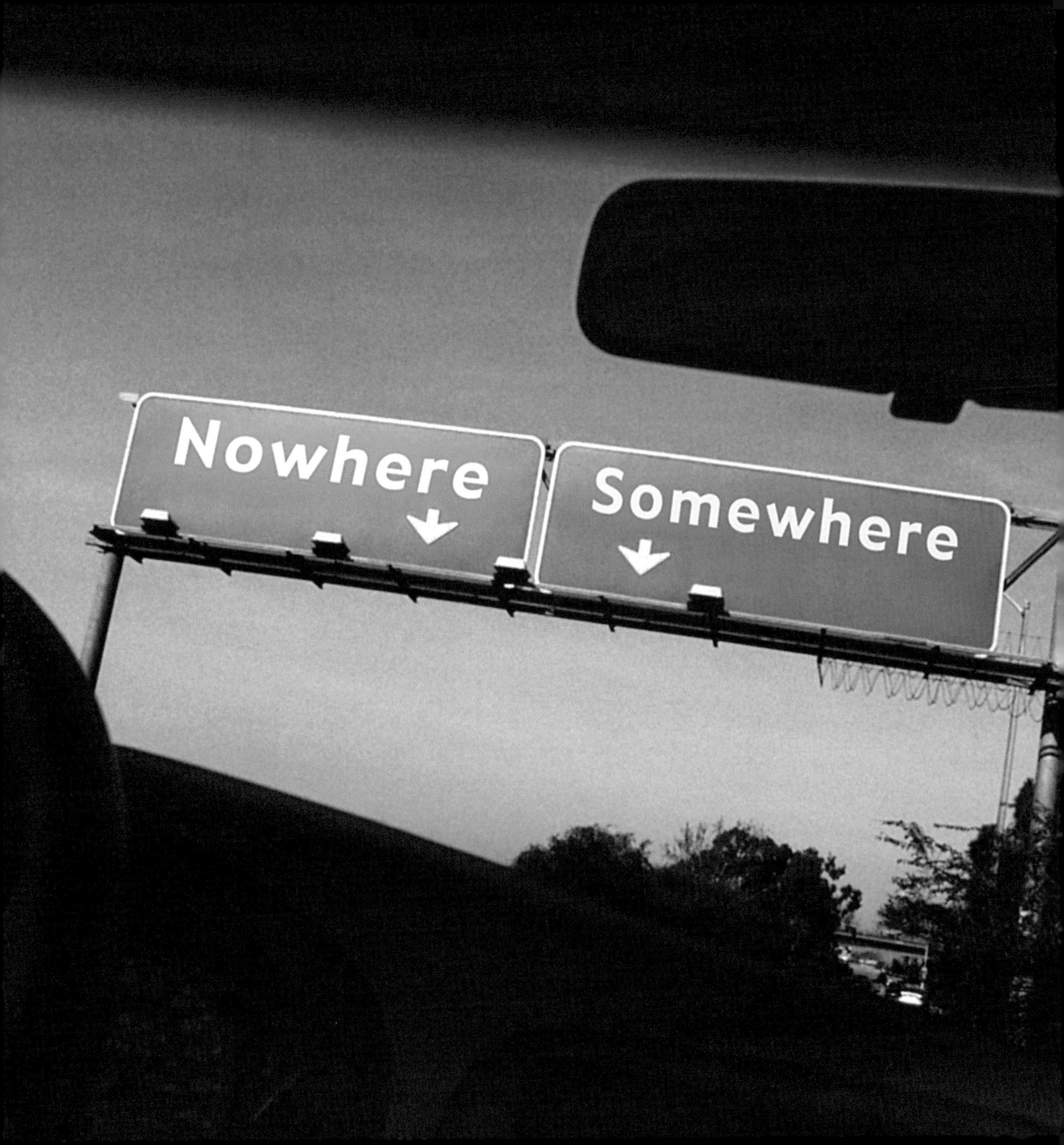
Nowhere
Somewhere

Prayer 65

Holy Master, God of Grace,
I believe: "ask and it shall be given you;
Seek, and ye shall find;
Knock, and it shall be opened unto you." [Matthew 7:7]
I seek you daily, Holy Master
For a closer walk in your grace. Amen.

Prayer 66

Father God,
Teach us to number our days
That we apply our hearts to wisdom. Amen.

Prayer 67

Dear God,
May we wake up tomorrow with a smile on our faces,
And may life hold us close with your love
and embrace your spirit.
May we experience happiness, friendship, gratitude, and peace. Amen.

Prayer 68

Dear God,
This child inside of me is a precious vessel
Pour into her heart tenderness and love
Incline her to understanding your word,
Give her compassion and kindness
Wrap her in your strength, perfect peace and joy.
Amen.

Prayer 69

Dear God,
In the presence of our Holy God,
Make my heart pure and my energies meek.
Help me to show mercy and be a peacemaker.
Allow me a change at the Alter and be always willing to listen and advise as I go to you
for answers. Allow me to be a calming presence in confusion.
Allow me to share comfort and a smile with all I meet.
Help me to nurture faith in my daily walk. Amen

Prayer 70

Father God,
We bless your Holy Name, Yahweh
You are always here when I need you most.
You are the friend, the father, the brother, and much more.
Today is the perfect day to thank you
For all the times you touched my heart
Thank you Father. Amen.

t away into ...
ountain ᵐwhere Jē'-ṡus had ap...
ointed them.

17 And when they saw him, they
worshipped him: but some doubted.
18 And Jē'-ṡus came and spake
unto them, saying, °All power is
given unto me in heaven and in earth.

tians of all ...
nations.
q Is. 52. 10.
Luke 24. 47.
Acts 2, 38, 39.
ᵐ ver. 7.
ch. 26. 32.
t Acts. 2. 42.
° Dan. 7. 13, 14.
ch. 11. 27.
Luke 1. 32.

20 ᵖTeaching the...
things whatsoever I ha...
ed you: and, lo, I am...
way, even unto th...
world. Ä'-mĕn.

THE GOSPEL ACCORDING TO

ST. MÄRK.

CHAPTER 1.

1 *The office of John the Baptist.* 9 *Jesus is
baptized,* 12 *tempted,* 14 *he preacheth:* 16
calleth Peter, Andrew, James and John:
23 *and healeth many.*

THE beginning of the gospel of
   Jē'-ṡus Christ, ᵇthe Son of God;
2 As it is written in the prophets,
ᵃBehold, I send my messenger before thy face, which shall prepare
thy way before thee.
3 ᶜThe voice of one crying in the
wilderness, Prepare ye the way of
the Lord, make his paths straight.
4 ᶠJohn did baptize in the wilderness, and preach the baptism of

A. D. 26.
ending.

³ or, cloven,
or, rent.
x Ps. 2. 7.
Mat. 3. 17.
ch. 9. 7.
ᵇ Mat. 14. 33.
Luke 1. 35.
John 1. 34.
ʸ Mat. 4. 1.
Luke 4. 1.
ᵈ Mal. 3. 1.
Mat. 11. 10.
Luke 7. 27.

ᶜ Is. 40. 3.
Mat. 3. 3.
Luke 3. 4.
John 1. 15,
23.
ᵃ Mat. 4. 11.
ᶠ Mat. 3. 1.
Luke 3. 3.
John 3. 23.
ᵇ Mat. 4. 12.
² or, unto.
ᶜ Mat. 4. 23.
ʰ Mat. 3. 5.

vens ³opened, a...
dove descendir...
11 And ther...
heaven, sayin...
loved Son,
pleased.
12 ʸAnd i...
driveth him...
13 And h...
derness f...
Sā'-tăn; ...
beasts; ...
unto hir...
14 ᵇNo...
in pris...
lēe, ...
kingd...
15 ...
filled

Prayer 71

Our Father, Most Holy One
Surround me with your love
Give your angels charge over me to keep me in righteous, safe protection
Allow me to be encouraging, stronger, and sharing.
In these challenging times help me to persevere with faith and love
Fill me with high values and compassion.
Make me a conveyor of holiness and joy. Amen.

Prayer 72

Holy Father,
May the love of my family reflect
Your eternal grace
May our devotion to life express holy praise to you, dear God. Amen.

Prayer 73

Our heavenly Father
Make me a generous spirit for the building of the tabernacle.
Place in me understanding, guidance, and caring to share with others.
Amen.

Prayer 74

Father God
These words may not often be spoken by me
Yet you are always remembered and you are first in my life
Thank you Father for my life. Amen

Prayer 75

Dear Father
As I learn to pray
I ask not for riches, fortune, nor fame,
I do believe you meet my needs as I bless your holy name.
Amen.

Prayer 76

God of the Universe
Your light years are not often seen
Even when they are always present,
Open our eyes to a higher learning of your knowledge. Amen.

Prayer 77

Dear Father
I seek you with all my heart.
"God also hath highly exalted Him,
And given him a name which is above every name." [Phillip 2:9]
I seek you with all my heart. Amen

Prayer 78

Father God
Bless our family with your gifts.
We believe every good gift
and every perfect gift is from above.
Bless you Father God. Amen.

Prayer 79

Our Father,
In the midst of our challenges we believe and have faith in the Lord
Father, you are a healer and our deliverer
In 2008, the year of new beginnings, we ask for the start of a continuous flow of your blessings into our home, just like those provided for the widow
In I Kings,
Open doors we cannot see and allow our entrance into the kingdom for eternal salvation,
Set in motion Malachi 3:10 many times over and over again.
Lord, be it your will, make your power flow 360 degrees to circumference our path, steadfast and unmovable always abiding in your word.
Grant us peace that it may spread throughout our community,
Grant us love that we may duplicate your trust and serve your will around the world,

Grant us humbleness to help all that are in need of your handiworks,
Abide us in faith, longsuffering, hope, and fervent prayer.
Thy will be done this day we pray. Amen.

Prayer 80

Most High Savior,
Your words are found and I did eat them.
I invite you into my life as the head of all my thoughts, plans, actions, works and visions, for righteous living,
Take hold of my inward parts for strength where there is weakness;
Show all that read this prayer today reconciliation as they recognize you dear God for your name sake.
We lift you up in the name of your only begotten Son.
Transform me into a vessel of your measure to be utilized
According to your riches and glory,
Make the end a vision realized and
A moral justice to serve many overlooked,
Make our enemies our footstool. Amen.

Prayer 81

Father, Father, Father,
Thank you for the breath of life when I could not breathe,
Thank you for 'The Vision' though a veil was before me,
Thank you for the gift of hearing The Word,
Oh what a comfort it has been.
Thank you for being the All in All to me:
The kindness, an expression of brotherly love,

A simple smile sent from above,
Thank you for your redeeming grace.
Where no man had power to reach the healing of my inner spirit,
Then, that spirit brought to remembrances of your love. Amen.

Prayer 82

Our Father
Expand my territory for your name sake
Protect me from evil and lead me to your holy place,
Amen.

Prayer 83

Father of Mercy,
Grace and Redemption,
Be always at the throne of my heart
And let there be praise continuous from my lips.
Amen.

Prayer 84

Dear Father,
In all my ways I acknowledge you.
Allow Obedience be continuous and made in my walk for the bond of brotherly love.
Amen.

Prayer 85

Lord and Savior Jesus Christ,
Through you we pray to our God in quiet oneness.
We stand on your word as promises are kept,
We obey your will,
We believe no weapon formed against us shall prosper,
We love you,
We thank you Father. Amen.

Prayer 86

God of All,
Quicken my spirit to unity, wisdom, and understanding of your word
With direction and guidance
I listen for your call. Amen

Prayer 87

God of All
Teach us to walk in the way of your Son
Forgiving and blessing those in need
Teach us how to train our children to follow you and walk in your word.
Guide us to encourage the youth and lead by positive example
Thank you for hearing our prayers. Amen.

Prayer 88

Jehovah, Yahweh –Blessed is He.
God of our forefathers Abraham, Isaac, and Jacob
From the lineage of Ruth you sent Yeshua (Jesus)
To fulfill the law, even from the womb of Mary, we thank you.
You chose us, Israel from our blessed heirs, we thank you.
Today, I choose you God in all your ways,
Your thoughts are so much higher than our thoughts and
We often do not understand the way.
Yet today, I choose you Father with full faith.
Anoint me in your wisdom and understanding to magnify your Holy name.
Forever I thank you. Amen.

Prayer 89

Our Father
When we approach the pinnacle of our salvation
Protect our mind and soul, protect our heart and protect our body.
Amen.

Prayer 90

God Almighty
We are down on bending knees
Prostrated in humbleness,
In formation, perpendicular to the square of righteousness
Our thanks to you God for sending one with a divine mind
One who gave of himself to elevate our weak links
One who energized momentum in the land and
Gave us a Royal blessing.
Forgive us Father for our faults and offenses with you,
Father with sincerity and deepest sorrow we ask your pardon
Cleanse us from our faults of omission and commission
Look down through time and summon us one by one
That we be found worthy to implement your will and Thy will be done.
Look into the seen and the unseen and continue to protect us
Implode in us a sharing spirit of Love, forever. Amen.

Prayer 91

Our Father
We thank thee for the willing hands and numerous and generous hearts who here do their work in full measure, pressed down and running over,
Who work not by the clock nor by the yardstick; not by the mere letter of the law, but who work because replicating your love vitalizes them.
Save us from using our offices and positions as a means for prestige.
Forgive us the stupidity that is deaf to the new and the different,
Not because they are bad, as we profess, but because we do not understand them and they therefore make us uncomfortable.
Forgive us, O' God that we are so easily tempted to "Lord it" over others.

Bridle our tongues lest we open our mouths only to reveal an empty head, an ugly spirit, or a heart of spite that knoweth not Thee.

Suffer us never to forget that the contentious and conceited spirit is the possession of small thinking women and petty men.

Save us the folly that worships at the altar of self; that looks in its mirror and repeats daily, without qualm, the mistakes of every yesterday.

Save us from obstinate refusal to learn our lessons.

Save us, lest, while we profess to be noble, we stand in the light of someone else.

Bestow on us, O' God, a lovely sense of humor, lest taking ourselves too seriously we shall be unable to see how ridiculous we appear to heaven and to earth, with our haughty looks and stiff necks.

Let not the spirit which magnifies or delights in failures of others, that uses the dagger of slander or the cutting of idle malicious words, be so much as known among us.

May the potentialities for good which thou hast planted in us, by the power, prosper. Help us to promote and protect them.

May our words and lives, in love and joy, in peace and goodness, in gentleness and patience, loyalty and faith, beautify life among us through Jesus Christ our Lord. Amen.

Prayer 92

Shalom Father,
Todah for this day,
May I be a blessing to you in deeds and truth.
Allow an awakening in our children to the sanctification of your word.
Build our faith while you utilize us to extend brotherly and sisterly love.
Amen.

Prayer 93

Our Father,
I will lift up mine eyes unto the hills, from whence cometh my help. My help cometh from the Lord, which made heaven and earth. He will not suffer thy foot to be moved; he that keepeth thee will not slumber.
Behold, he that keepeth Israel shall neither slumber nor sleep.
The Lord is thy keeper; the Lord is thy shade upon thy right hand.
The sun shall not spite thee by day, nor the moon by night. The Lord shall preserve thee from all evil; he shall preserve thy soul
The Lord shall preserve thy going out and thy coming in from this time forth, and even for evermore.   [*Psalms 121*]
Amen.

Prayer 94

Our Father, we pray:
Behold, bless ye the Lord all ye servants of the Lord, which by night stand in the house of the Lord.
Lift up your hands in the sanctuary, and bless the Lord.
The lord that made heaven and earth bless thee out of Zion. [*Psalms 94*]
Amen.

Prayer 95

Our Father,
Lord lay me down to sleep, I pray the Lord my soul to keep.
If I die before I wake, I pray the Lord my soul to take. Amen.

Prayer 96

Our Father,
Help us to know sin is a form of death.
Help us to know sin is **SeperatIoN** from God
Help us to recognize when we walk into sin, step by step, that we may
Turn from that direction.
Help us to see quickly that we may turn away from deceivers, and go out of sin by seeking God daily, continuous, with obedience, determination, commitment and assertiveness.
Help us to know if we fall, to get up and return to the race of life with God.
Help us to know who Jesus is, and who you are God.
Help us to know John 3:16 "For God so loved the world that he gave his only begotten Son, that whosoever believeth in him should not perish, but have everlasting life"
Help us to know who we are in relation to you and our true history.
Help us to know our purpose in life and to reach the fullness of our purpose in such a way to hear you say well done, thy good and faithful servant.
Keep us steadfast, unmovable, and always about our Fathers business.
Keep us and teach us line upon line and precept upon precept your way seeking the higher calling forever and evermore. Amen.

Prayer 97

Father, Father, Father,
Protect us until we meet again,
Put away from us a forward mouth, and perverse lips. Protect us from liars and false witness bearing statements of partial facts.
Make your way straight in our hearts that we may always speak truth.
Until we meet again, May the wind be at our back and God hold us gently in the palm of His hand. Amen.

Prayer 98

Our Father,

You are omnipotent to us, we thank you and bless your holy name.

Peter said you are the Sheep Shepherd, John said you are the Good Shepherd, Paul referred to you as the Great Shepherd.

In Genesis you were the seed of a woman

In Exodus you are the Passover lamb

In Leviticus you are the high priest

In Numbers you are the pillar of cloud by day and the pillar of fire by night,

In Deuteronomy you are a prophet like Moses

In Joshua you are the captain of our salvation

In Judges you are the judge and law giver

In Ruth you are the kinman redeemed

In first and second Samuel you are the trusted prophet

In Kings and Chronicles you are the reigning King

In Ezra you are the rebuilder of the broken down wall of human life

In Esther you are the mordecai

In Job you are ever giving redeemed

In Psalms you are the Shepherd

In Proverbs you are the Bride Groom

In Isaiah you are the Prince of Peace

In Jeremiah you are the righteous branch

In Lamentation you are the weeping prophet

In Ezekiel you are the wonderful full face man

In Daniel you are the fourth man in Lots fiery furnace

In Hosea you are the faithful husband forever **mending** to backsliders

In Joel you are the baptizer with the holy ghost and with fire

In Amos you are the burden down

In Obadiah you are mighty to save

In Jonah you are the great foreign missionary
In Michael you are the messenger with beautiful feet
In Nahum you are the avenger of God's Elect
In Habakkuk you are God's Evangelist crying for a revival
In Zedekiah you are saved
You are more than saved to us:
In Matthew you are the Messiah
In Mark you are the wonder wisher
In Luke you are the Son of Man
In John you are the Son of God
In Acts you are the Holy Ghost
In Romans you are our justifier
In first and second Corinthians you are the sanctifier
In Galatians you are the redeemer from the curse of the law
In Ephesians you are Christ of searchable riches
In Philippians you are the God who supply all our needs
In Colossians you are fullest of Godhead embodiment
In first and second Thessalonians you are soon coming King
In first and second Timothy He's our mediator between God and man.
Thank you Father for being the same yesterday, today, and tomorrow.
Amen. [*Compliments of Reverend Brown*]

Prayer 99

Our Father,
We rest in your bosom, at the feet of Jesus
Where divine blessings flow. Early in my days we were told
Ninety-nine and a half (99 ½) will not due to be worthy for the kingdom
Of heaven. We continue to seek you by sending out to the ether "come to know God",
the Good News of your Son, Messiah teachings as a model life, on our journey as we
strive to make it In. Our focus is to enter in at the straight and narrow gate, giving and
sharing 110% and more. We sometimes call our efforts 111—one for the Father, one for
the Son, and one for the Holy Spirit.
Elevating one iota in ancient knowledge we have come to know the number eight (8) is
new beginning—and that new beginning comes in every breath we take. We welcome
the new beginning to learn of you because of who you are dear God. We pray to be
made free indeed. We forgive our brothers 70 times 7. We thank you for sharing your
wondrous wisdom brought to us by many great teachers with cross cultural origins,
among them are doctors of divinity, ministers of truth, instructors and leaders of the
Nation, Sunday school theologians, elders, educators and writers.
We have marked time. You have kept The Promise. Because of you we know our true
history, we thank you.
Abba for your eternal love, for infinite wisdom, for our lives and brotherly love, for our
families and our friends, we thank you.
For our acquaintances and all the Angels you sent along the way,
For three measures of meal prepared to rise for God's Great Cause,
For the blood on the door post, for the circumcision,
For the Sacrificial Cross and the Altar, we thank you.
All of **me** have reciprocated to **we for us** eternally, by faith
In unity, we thank you. Amen. (*Prayer for YBY*)

Prayer 100

Our Father

We have come to the pause of our journey

If you allowed a few words to be given to each reader

And if we were chosen, we would share concerning God…

"Thou shalt love the Lord thy God with all your heart, and with all your soul,

And with all your strength, and with all your mind;

And love your neighbor as yourself. [St Luke 10]

"Trust in the Lord with all thine heart; and lean not unto thine own understanding.

In all thy ways acknowledge Him, and He shall direct thy paths.

Be not wise in thine own eyes: fear the Lord, and depart from evil.

It shall be health to thy navel, and 'marrow' to thy bones.

Honor the Lord with thy substance, and with the first fruits of all thine increase..."

[Proverbs 3:5-9]

Amen, amen, amen.

Post Script: In the beginning of this book we wrote of a variable language and dialect having a least common denominator which you will find in your proper environment and respective time. We believe the denominator to be, ACTION. Take each word you speak in prayer for the right and reasonable service then ACT on it, step toward God, hold to the Truth, and in the quiet wait of your reality is the substance of your being. For my people: "Those who are called by HIS name, if you would humble yourselves, pray and turn from wicked ways, then HE WILL heal the land."
"May God Bless and keep you until we meet again."

REFERENCES

1. **Molahs** is a right to left reading of **Shalom**. Meant only to replicate English Shalom, Implicates a return to God. No other meaning should be applied for world languages.

2. Daily Word 1982, Our Daily Bread 2000. Taken from Our Daily Bread, Copyright 2010 by RBC Ministries, Grand Rapids, MI. Reprinted by permission. All rights reserved.

3. Reproduced from, "Wisdom In the Hebrew Alphabet " by "Rabbi Michael Munk" with permission from the copyright holders ARTSCROLL/MESORAH Publications, LTD

4. Adult Bible Studies, United Methodist Publishing House (2007 by Cokesbury)

5. Holy Bible, King James Version, Zondervan, *ISBN recorded*

6. Holy Bible, New International Version, *ISBN recorded*

7. Webster Collegiate Dictionary and Documentary Research

8. Bible Study Course Presentations: FBC, Yahweh Books, Christian Studies, COGIC

9. Civilization Lectures

10. Consult your Bible where scripture is referenced for exact phrase, words, subjects and punctuation.

Marilyn,
Neda, Mary

Otis, Mary,
Reece

Willie

Willie Mae, Henrietta
White, The Twins

Your Notes

Order Molahs Shalom music CD from Http://www.Until*I*LearnToPray.com

LaVergne, TN USA
25 March 2011
221535LV00002B